A POWERFUL PRAYER APPROACH

Six phases of life-changing
intimacy with God.

TRACY HATCH

Founder, OneTen Ministries

A Powerful Prayer Approach
Six phases of life-changing intimacy with God.

Copyright © 2023, Tracy Hatch
First Edition
Published by Metamorphoō Press, Prior Lake, Minnesota.

ISBN 979-8-9885706-0-8 (paperback)
ISBN 979-8-9885706-1-5 (eBook)

Theological review provided by Pastor Jason Foreman, M. Div., Trinity Evangelical Divinity School.

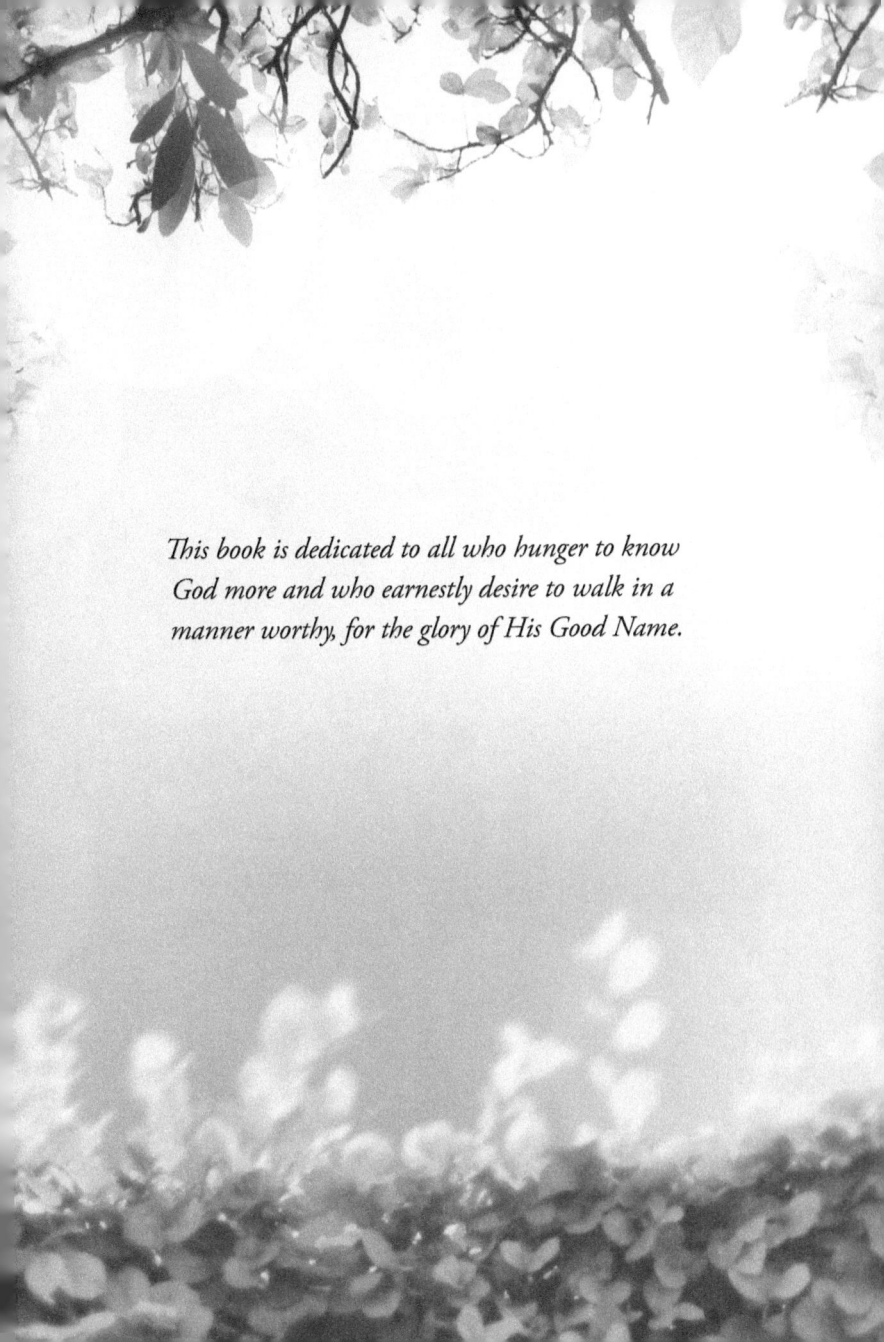

This book is dedicated to all who hunger to know God more and who earnestly desire to walk in a manner worthy, for the glory of His Good Name.

CONTENTS

CHAPTER 1

WHY PRAY?

Be still, and know that I am God!

PSALM 46:10A

Do you ever struggle with prayer? Do you feel like your prayers aren't powerful? Do you ever wonder if you're "doing it right"?

Let me assure you that every Christian has felt this way. You are not alone, and you no longer have to struggle with an ineffective prayer life.

Some religious orders lead people to believe God only hears prayers from those with certain titles or positions. This is not biblically accurate.

Many people believe one must use fancy or eloquent-sounding words to pray effectively. Also not true, Jesus Himself refuted this idea (Matthew 6:5-13).

The truth is that everyone can pray—no fancy title, elaborate attire, or special words needed. Prayer is simply a conversation of love between you and the God of the universe. Don't let that frighten you, though. The Bible says that God delights in you, His masterpiece, and He seeks a relationship with you (Ephesians 2:10). He invites you to come to Him, and He indeed hears your prayers (Matthew 11:28; Hebrews 4:16).

While there is no set formula for prayer, there are powerful elements found in many of the prayers recorded in Scripture. We can learn from these prayers, and other Scripture, to turn our everyday prayers into a conversation closer to the heart of God.

Even though God hears your prayers, He is not a genie in a bottle just waiting around to grant your every wish. He doesn't owe you an answer to your prayer. There isn't a magic formula to ensure your prayers are answered as you expect. But there is a framework we can use to approach God and create a genuine connection with the heart of our Heavenly Father. This connection, and the intimacy within that connectedness, is powerful. Sometimes this intimacy moves His heart to provide. Sometimes the Holy Spirit moves your heart to ask for the blessing of others above yourself. Often this deep communion with God changes your heart, your will, and your requests. If done genuinely and with the right motive, communion with God in prayer will change your life!

Powerful prayer is about a heart yielded to Him. If that is what you seek, then this book is for you!

On the following pages you will find a powerful approach to deep intimacy with God that is easy to remember and implement in your life right now. Each of the six phases of the prayer begin with the letter 'A': *Align, Adore, Appreciate, Acknowledge, Ask* and *Act*.

I pray that you, and your relationship with God, will be forever changed as you connect more deeply with His heart.

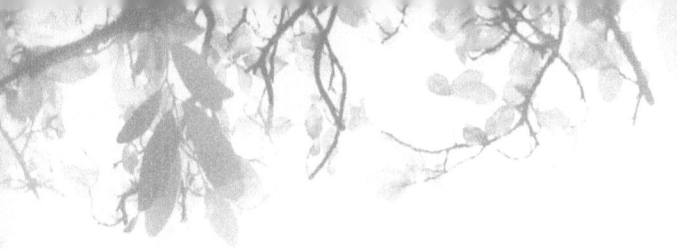

CHAPTER 2

ALIGN

Submit yourselves therefore to God.

JAMES 4:7A ESV

This first phase of prayer, *Align*, and the last phase, *Act*, serve as bookends for the main prayer components. In the *Align* phase, we approach God with the recognition that His will is our best outcome, and we seek to align all that we are with Him and His perfect plan.

The whole self is made up of the body, spirit, and soul. The body is the physical part of one's being. The spirit of a person is the God-breathed essence of life, the part that makes one truly alive. The soul consists of a person's mind, will, and emotions.

To align with someone or some idea is "to array on the side of" or "to bring into or be in line" with something.[1] This is precisely what we want to do in this first phase of prayer. Begin your time with God by intentionally choosing to align your spirit, soul, and body with the living God.

James gives us a nice example of declaring alignment at the beginning of his book. James, who was Jesus' biological half-brother (same mother, different father), declares that he is a "servant of God and of the Lord Jesus Christ" (James 1:1 ESV). Although he grew up with Jesus and knew Jesus well, he asserts his submission to Jesus as a servant. James clearly declared his alignment.

Even Jesus begins His prayers with alignment by saying, "My Father." This demonstrates a posture of submission and alignment under Father God's authority. Jesus chose to acknowledge His Father's authority and, though Jesus was fully God, voluntarily submitted to that authority.

An alignment prayer can be as simple as:

> *Oh God, I love You and I seek to do Your will. I command my spirit, soul, and body to align with Your sovereign will.*

Or:

> *Indeed LORD, I come before You this day and I submit to You as **my** Lord. I therefore intentionally align all that I am and all that I have underneath Your righteous authority.*

Or something more elaborate, such as:

Heavenly Father,

It is in Your name and under Your authority that I come. Just as our Lord Jesus is perfectly in alignment with You and Your will, and the Holy Spirit is perfectly in alignment with Jesus, I, too, seek alignment with Your will and the truth You have provided through Scripture. I now commit my whole self to You: spirit, soul, and body.

In the name and authority of the Lord Jesus Christ, I command my spirit to come into alignment with the Holy Spirit.

In the name and authority of the Lord Jesus Christ, I command my soul (my mind, will, and emotions) to come into alignment with my spirit, which is in alignment with the Holy Spirit.

In the name and authority of the Lord Jesus Christ, I command my body to come into alignment with my soul and the Holy Spirit.

Lord God, keep all of me in perfect alignment with Your Holy Spirit.

I further consecrate myself, my thoughts, and my

mind to You alone. May only thoughts ordained by You be present in our time together.

By the authority of the Name of Jesus I pray,

Amen.[2]

WHAT TO DO WHEN ALIGNMENT IS HARD

What happens if you aren't in alignment with God as you begin your prayer time? When your heart is hurting and your mind is racing over a pain or hurt you have experienced, it can be difficult to genuinely come before God and release your desire to get what you want (e.g., vindication, your idea of justice, restitution, or recompense)? It might be hard to imagine that there could be any way to look at your situation other than how you see it. In times like these, it might be hard to honestly come before God at the beginning of your prayer time and lay down your will to align under His. When that happens, it's ok to admit that you *want* to come into alignment under His Spirit and authority, but your heart may not be ready.

Jesus once encountered a man who was trying but needed some help in a similar way. The interaction is recorded in Mark 9. A man brought his son to Jesus for healing yet his fear and uncertainty were obstacles to his faith. He said to Jesus, "I believe, help my unbelief." Jesus did not scold the man or send him away; He recognized where the man was and had compassion on him. Jesus still healed the man's son. Jesus wants us to come to Him in our honest state and work through our unbelief with Him rather than not come to Him at all.

I believe He feels the same way about our alignment. If you're struggling, still come to Him and ask for help in your struggle. Your prayer may be something like this:

> *Lord, I love You. I want to perfectly align my will and my spirit under Yours, but my heart is heavy today. Please help my mind, will, and emotions to come into alignment with Yours during our time together. I lay my hurt at Your feet, and I ask for Your help, so that I may faithfully follow You.*

This alignment action is intended to focus your entire being on Him as you submit to His will and gently remind the self-centered parts of you that His will is better than yours.

Before you begin to pray, take a moment to quiet your heart before the Lord. Welcome the Holy Spirit into your prayer time and space as you align your spirit, soul (mind, will, and emotions), and body under the authority of God and His faithful love.

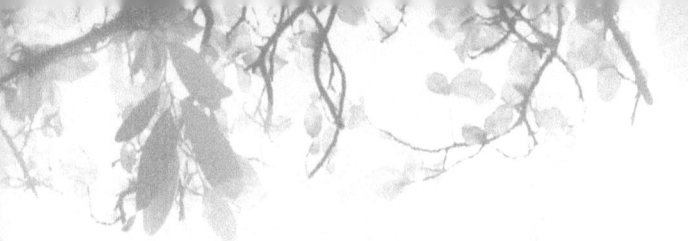

CHAPTER 3

ADORE

Come, let us worship and bow down.
Let us kneel before the LORD our Maker.

PSALM 95:6

To adore something or someone is "to worship or honor as a deity or as divine; to regard with loving admiration and devotion." This word in particular, as compared to its synonyms, "implies love and stresses the notion of an individual and personal attachment."[3] In this phase we take time to focus on worshiping God, not for what He can do or has done for us—that will come later—but to worship Him for *who* He is.

The best way to know the nature of God is to study His Word. Through His Word we learn that among His many attributes, He is patient, loving, merciful, good, just, and kind. He is endless, and therefore our reasons to adore Him are also endless. While we don't need to be afraid to approach God (Hebrews 4:16), we should still approach Him with reverence and respect (Hebrews 12:28).

I love what Job's friend, Elihu, says in Job 36:3 (ESV), "I will get my knowledge from afar and ascribe righteousness to my Maker." This was an anchor point for the rest of Elihu's discourse. He declared that his quest for answers and meaning start by recognizing who God really is, at least as much of Him as we humans can understand.

Too often we rush through our prayers, and even our days, without really taking time to think carefully about who God is. We are so used to Him being there whenever we have time for Him, that we develop a much too casual approach to the All Powerful, All Knowing, Creator of the Universe. When we begin our prayer time focusing our minds on who God really is, our minds and hearts come to rest in the peace and assurance that He is on His throne, and at His disposal is every resource we could ever need.

In this phase of prayer, focus on worshipping God for Himself. Let your heart and mind worship Him with awe and wonder as you consider His attributes (Psalm 46:10; Luke 10:27). Use the various names or attributes of God as you worship. This helps to focus your mind and set the stage for the next phase.

Here is a list of just some of the attributes of God. You may want to use these attributes in your worship. He is:

- Self-existent
- Eternal
- Good
- Omniscient (all-knowing)
- Omnipresent (always present)
- Omnipotent (all-powerful)
- Immutable (unchanging)
- Holy
- Love
- Righteous
- Just
- Truth
- Faithful
- Compassionate
- Merciful
- Gracious
- Sovereign

Here is a list of just some of the names of God that you may also want to use in your prayers:

- El (The Strong One)
- Elohim (Creator God)
- Jehovah (Lord, the Self-Existent One)
- Adonai (Master)
- El Shaddai (Almighty God)
- El Elyon (The Most High God)
- El Olam (The God of All Ages)
- Jehovah Jireh (The Lord Will Provide)
- El Roi (The God Who Sees Me)
- El Nose (The God Who Forgives)
- El Emunah (The Faithful God)
- Jehovah Rapha (The Lord that Heals)
- Jehovah Nissi (The Lord my Banner)
- Jehovah Shalom (The Lord my Peace)

Music is also a powerful way to create the right atmosphere as you enter a time of adoration. Choose songs that focus on His attributes and character.

The Psalms recorded in the Bible are ancient songs and

have been used for millennia to express adoration for God. You can read the Psalms as devotions or use them as your prayers. Here are just a few examples:

- Psalm 92:1-9
- Psalm 93
- Psalms 95-100
- Psalms 103-105

Adoration prayers could be as simple as saying something like:

> *LORD God, I worship You and adore You. I come before You, and I praise You for who You are. You are the only Sovereign One, the Creator of the Universe.*

Or you could pray a more elaborate prayer such as:

> *LORD God, I worship You and adore You. I come before You, and I praise You for who You are. You are El Emunah, my faithful God. You are my joy and my delight. I love You, and I seek to know You more. I praise You because You alone are worthy. You alone are good and gracious, slow to anger and abounding in steadfast love....*

Go ahead, adore Him. Give Him adoration and praise, for He is so worthy. Sit in awe of His majesty and grace, marvel at His love and faithfulness. Bow before Him humbly, declare His rightful place on the throne of the universe as well as your heart.

CHAPTER 4

Appreciate

*Oh give thanks to the L*ORD*, for He is good;*
for His steadfast love endures forever!

1 Chronicles 16:34 esv

No matter what you have or wish you had, no matter what you're going through at this moment, there are still many reasons to be grateful. Sometimes we forget and take for granted the good things in life because the hard things seem to demand more attention. Yet when we take time to pause and consider our blessings, we realize we have much cause for gratitude.

Gratitude is a bit of a buzz word these days. People talk about gratitude in a general sense, keep gratitude journals, and even spend thousands of dollars on retreats to help them develop a lifestyle of gratitude. However, the popular gratitude craze often misses the most critical component of gratitude — the *One* to whom our gratitude is due. Ephesians 5:20 says to "give thanks for everything to God the Father in the name of our Lord Jesus Christ."

To appreciate is to "grasp the nature, worth, quality, or significance of; to value or admire highly; to recognize with gratitude.[4]" While our human minds cannot fully grasp the worth, nature, and full significance of Almighty God, we can thank Him and praise Him for what we can understand.

Take time during your prayers to give thanks to God for who He is, all He has done, and all He has provided. Give thanks to God for His faithfulness and that He is slow to anger. Give thanks to God for all the challenges you have not had to go through. And, yes, even give thanks to Him for all the hard things in life, including the hard things you are still going through. He has a way of redeeming even our hardest moments and deepest pain when we offer them back to Him in faith.

There are many Scriptures that can aid you in developing a habit of appreciation. Here are just a few:

> Give thanks to the LORD and proclaim His greatness.
>   Let the whole world know what He has done.
> Sing to Him; yes, sing His praises.
>   Tell everyone about His wonderful deeds.
>   (Psalm 105:1-2)

It is good to give thanks to the LORD,
  to sing praises to the Most High.
It is good to proclaim Your unfailing love in the morning,
  Your faithfulness in the evening (Psalm 92:1-2)

Let all that I am praise the LORD;
  may I never forget the good things He does for me.
He forgives all my sins
  and heals all my diseases.

He redeems me from death
  and crowns me with love and tender mercies.
He fills my life with good things.
      (Psalm 103:2-5a)

In this phase of prayer, spend some time in a posture of gratitude, thanking God for all your blessings. Even if there is a need or if there are challenges in your life, there are still reasons to be grateful to Him, the Giver of all good things (James 1:17 ESV). Name those things for which you are thankful. Give Him gratitude because He knows you, understands your struggles, and has good plans for you and your future (Jeremiah 29:11).

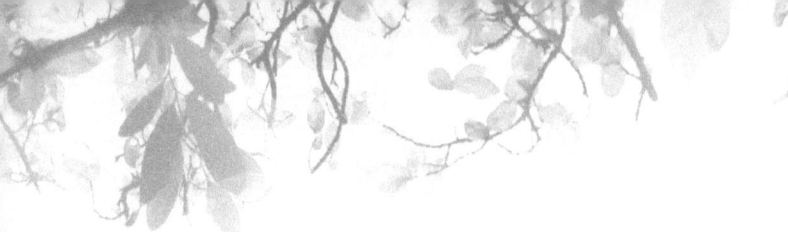

CHAPTER 5

ACKNOWLEDGE

*So let us come boldly to the throne of our gracious
God. There we will receive His mercy, and we
will find grace to help us when we need it most.*

HEBREWS 4:16

Acknowledging is the hardest and most transformative phase of prayer. This phase encompasses multiple elements that expand and deepen your prayer life.

To acknowledge is to:

- "recognize the rights, authority, or status of;

- disclose knowledge of or agreement with;

- express gratitude or obligation for;

- take notice of;

- make known the receipt of;
- recognize as genuine or valid.[5]"

Therefore, in this phase you will:

1. Recognize the rights, authority, or status of God (1 Chronicles 29:11-13).

2. Disclose (confess) knowledge of any sin in your life—willful or accidental—and your sorrow for sinning (Psalm 19:12-13). Then, commit to turning away from sin. Be sure to include any agreement you have had with any form of spiritual darkness, such as the use of crystals, talking to the dead, use of Ouija boards, etc. (Acts 26:18).

3. Express gratitude to God for who He is and that He has chosen you to be in a love relationship with Him (especially if you did not include the previous *Appreciate* phase in your prayer) (Psalm 100:3).

4. Declare (take notice) that Jesus is The Savior and Lord (Matthew 16:15-16).

5. Admit your receipt of His grace and forgiveness (Psalm 103:12).

6. Express recognition that God genuinely has all authority, power, and dominion (1 Chronicles 29:11-13; Ephesians 1:18-23).

Don't neglect the full confession of your sin (Proverbs 14:9). Scripture says that unconfessed sin can be a barrier which prevents God from fully hearing your prayers (Proverbs 28:9; 1 Peter 3:7).

Start by humbling yourself before Him (Matthew 23:12). Then examine your heart (Psalm 139:23-24). Be honest about the way you have strayed from His perfect plan. Confess your sins: the ungodly thoughts, the words you said or didn't say, and the actions you did or didn't do (Psalm 51). Acknowledge your sincerity to turn from your sins and, with His strength, endeavor to live a righteous life (Matthew 5:6; Matthew 6:33). Recognize Jesus' sacrifice which allows you to take your place as a forgiven, beloved child of God (1 John 1:9). Then, acknowledge and accept that He has forgiven you, just as His word says He does if you have put your faith and trust in Jesus as your Lord and Savior.

In this phase you can also speak honestly with God about your challenges, concerns, fears, and struggles. Don't be afraid to be honest yet respectful with Him. He knows your heart and mind; He knows your situation and challenges. He is not surprised or upset when you bring your hard things to Him. He loves you and wants to help you.

Please don't let this phase overwhelm you. To put it simply, you will acknowledge your sin and your hurt. You will acknowledge that He is God, and you are not. Acknowledge your need of Him and your love for Him. Acknowledge your rightful inheritance now that you are saved by grace through your faith in Jesus Christ.

Reinforce your alignment by acknowledging that God has the final say and the authority to rightfully have His way.

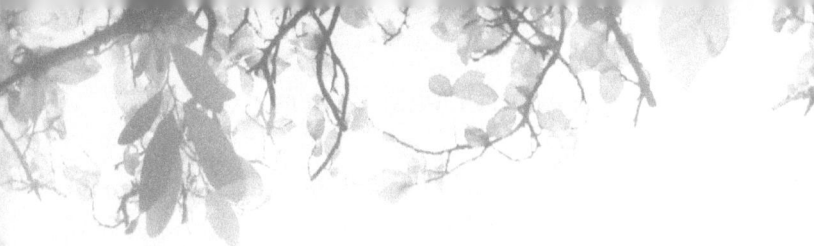

CHAPTER 6

ASK

Do not be anxious about anything, but in
every situation, by prayer and petition, with
thanksgiving, present your requests to God.

PHILIPPIANS 4:6 NIV

Most people's minds automatically default to this phase when they think of prayer. In this phase, you will present your needs and the needs of others to God.

For reasons we may not know on this side of eternity, God has chosen to partner with us to bring forward blessing, healing, and peace upon the earth. While He can, and does, act all on His own, He also has established a role for us. Something powerful happens when we present our requests to God and partner with Him to see our needs met and our world changed.

In John 4:10, Jesus says to the Samaritan woman, "If you only knew the gift God has for you and who you are speaking to, you would ask Me…" I love this bold idea. We have no idea the gifts God has for us or what He wants to give us. We just need to go to Him and ask.

So, do not be afraid to ask. He already knows your heart and your needs. Ask Him to show you His heart and His plans for your situation. Ask Him to intervene and do what only He can do!

Intercede for others by asking that He meet their needs. If you have a health challenge—ask Him! If you have a financial challenge—ask Him! If you have a relationship need—ask Him! Inquire of the Lord regarding His plans, where He is at work, and your role in coming alongside Him to impact your life and the world around you. Ask Him to be with you and to give you strength and wisdom. Ask Him to draw the people you love to come to know, love, and follow Jesus as their Lord and Savior. Ask Him to heal your community and your nation. The list really is endless!

Remember that He has unlimited resources (1 Chronicles 29:11-12; Psalm 50). There is no ask too big or too small. He loves you and wants to grant you every request made in alignment with His perfect will (Psalm 37:4). Ask with humble expectancy, then watch to see how God moves after you pray. *(See the chapter titled "How to Use This Book" for additional ideas.)*

CHAPTER 7

ACT

*Just as the body is dead without breath, so
also faith is dead without good works.*

JAMES 2:26

J ust like Scripture says that faith without works is dead
(James 2:26), prayer without action is incomplete. To act
is to do just what it says, to take action.[6] There is even a book
in the New Testament named *Acts* or *The Acts of the Apostles*
precisely because it records the actions taken by the apostles
as a result of prayer. In many places the book describes the
apostles being in prayer and then sensing the Holy Spirit
leading them to take a particular action, with which they
promptly complied.

As you pray, pay attention to the subtle nudging of the
Holy Spirit. He will never ask you to do anything contrary to

Scripture or the nature of God, but He often asks us to put our faith in action. He may ask you to call someone, apologize to someone, or give something. Act in alignment with God's word, His character, and His definition of righteousness.

God will never contradict His Word. He will never want you to act in a way that is inconsistent with the letter and Spirit of the whole counsel of Scripture, the Holy Bible. So, anything you believe He is asking you to do as an action after prayer will always be consistent with His nature and His Word.

Let your time with Him in prayer influence your thoughts, words, and actions for the rest of the day.

Sometimes, the actions appear to make no human sense. But God's ways are not our ways, and His thoughts are not our thoughts (Isaiah 55:9). His ideas are bigger and better than ours. He sees a much bigger picture, and He sees the future. He may ask you to do something that you would not have ever considered. If it is something significant, pray about it again and ask a Christian pastor, mentor, or friend to pray as well. Pray for additional discernment or the right opportunity. If needed, ask Him to help you in your unbelief and provide you with some revelation or circumstance to confirm what you believe He is telling you to do.

If we pray but never act when prompted by the Holy Spirit in prayer, we will never experience the full joy of our relationship with Him, and we will all miss out on blessings He is ready to provide.

Pay attention to the Spirit's promptings. Validate that the promptings are from God by being consistent with His nature and His Word and by the peace and strength you receive from the Holy Spirit to carry the action out. And then act without delay.

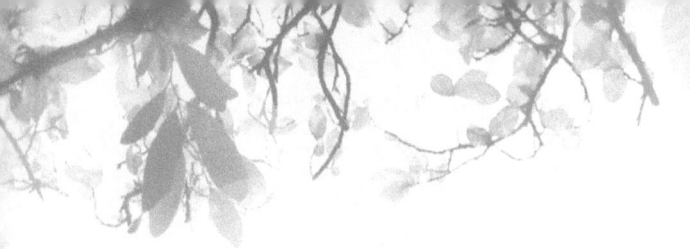

CHAPTER 8

BIBLICAL EXAMPLES

*Follow God's example, therefore, as
dearly loved children.*

EPHESIANS 5:1 NIV

There are many great prayers in the Bible that serve as examples for us to enrich our own prayer lives. In this chapter, we will briefly examine some of my favorite prayers. You will see that this prayer approach is as ancient as Scripture itself yet as applicable today as it was then.

THE LORD'S PRAYER

Jesus' own teaching on prayer is recorded in Luke 11 and Matthew 6. In the sermon on the mount recorded in Matthew 6, Jesus said,

[9]Pray like this:
Our Father in heaven,
   may your name be kept holy.
[10]May your Kingdom come soon.
May your will be done on earth,
   as it is in heaven.
[11]Give us today the food we need
[12]and forgive us our sins,
   as we have forgiven those who sin against us.
[13]And don't let us yield to temptation
   but rescue us from the evil one.

He went on to say:

[14]If you forgive those who sin against you, your heavenly Father will forgive you. [15]But if you refuse to forgive others, your Father will not forgive your sins.

Now, notice the elements of this prayer approach in each segment of the prayer:

1. *Our Father in heaven*

    Align: Jesus recognizes that God is our Father, representing an authority over us, and that

He is higher than us. We acknowledge our intentional alignment under the headship and authority of God right at the outset.

2. *may your name be kept holy.*

> **Adore:** Jesus is noting an important attribute of God — that He is Holy and His name represents His Holiness. This is worship and adoration of the nature of God.

3. *May your Kingdom come soon. May your will be done on earth, as it is in heaven.*

> **Appreciate:** Jesus is teaching us to recognize God's ultimate dominion over everything and to declare that God's will is higher than our will. His authority and His wisdom exceed that of our own and is worthy of our appreciation and gratitude.

4. *Give us today the food we need*

> **Ask:** Jesus gives us permission to ask God for what we need daily. While this verse specifically refers to food, this is widely understood to mean all provision.

5. *and forgive us our sins, as we have forgiven those who sin against us.*

> **Acknowledge and Act:** Jesus was sinless, yet He knew that we would need daily forgiveness of sins. He also included an action for us within the prayer: that we would likewise forgive others. *Note that in Jesus' prayer this Acknowledge section follows the Ask section.*

6. *If you forgive those who sin against you, your heavenly Father will forgive you. But if you refuse to forgive others, your Father will not forgive your sins.*

> **Act:** Jesus follows His prayer with an admonition to follow-through on our action to forgive. In verse 12, we prayed to be forgiven and acknowledged that we will be forgiven to the degree we forgive others. Here, Jesus underscores the importance of actually doing what we have prayed.

DANIEL'S PRAYER

Daniel is an Old Testament prophet who was known by Jews as well as by the secular leaders for his great faith and devotion to God. The book of Daniel chronicles his difficult early life and how he remained faithful to God regardless of his very difficult circumstances. Chapter nine records Daniel's famous prayer of repentance on behalf of the people of Israel, and his plea to God for which God dispatches the angel Gabriel in response. Now that is a powerful prayer!

Daniel 9:4-19:

> [4] I prayed to the LORD my God and confessed: "O Lord, You are a great and awesome God! You always fulfill Your covenant and keep Your promises of unfailing love to those who love You and obey Your commands. [5] But we have sinned and done wrong. We have rebelled against You and scorned Your commands and regulations. [6] We have refused to listen to Your servants the prophets, who spoke on Your authority to our kings and princes and ancestors and to all the people of the land.

> [7] Lord, You are in the right; but as You see, our faces are covered with shame. This is true of all of us, including the people of Judah and Jerusalem and all Israel, scattered near and far, wherever You have driven us because of our disloyalty to You. [8] O LORD, we and our kings, princes, and ancestors are covered with shame because

we have sinned against You. [9] But the Lord our God is merciful and forgiving, even though we have rebelled against Him. [10] We have not obeyed the LORD our God, for we have not followed the instructions He gave us through His servants the prophets. [11] All Israel has disobeyed Your instruction and turned away, refusing to listen to Your voice.

So now the solemn curses and judgments written in the Law of Moses, the servant of God, have been poured down on us because of our sin. [12] You have kept Your word and done to us and our rulers exactly as You warned. Never has there been such a disaster as happened in Jerusalem. [13] Every curse written against us in the Law of Moses has come true. Yet we have refused to seek mercy from the LORD our God by turning from our sins and recognizing His truth. [14] Therefore, the LORD has brought upon us the disaster He prepared. The LORD our God was right to do all of these things, for we did not obey Him.

[15] O Lord our God, You brought lasting honor to Your name by rescuing Your people from Egypt in a great display of power. But we have sinned and

are full of wickedness. [16] In view of all Your faithful mercies, Lord, please turn Your furious anger away from Your city Jerusalem, Your holy mountain. All the neighboring nations mock Jerusalem and Your people because of our sins and the sins of our ancestors.

[17] O our God, hear Your servant's prayer! Listen as I plead. For Your own sake, Lord, smile again on Your desolate sanctuary.

[18] O my God, lean down and listen to me. Open Your eyes and see our despair. See how Your city—the city that bears Your name—lies in ruins. We make this plea, not because we deserve help, but because of Your mercy.

[19] O Lord, hear. O Lord, forgive. O Lord, listen and act! For Your own sake, do not delay, O my God, for Your people and your city bear your name."

Here is how the framework shows up in Daniel's prayer:

1. *O Lord*

> **Align:** Daniel declares God's Lordship over his life.

2. *You are a great and awesome God!*

> **Adore:** Daniel rightly praises God by proclaiming that He is great and awesome.

3. *You always fulfill Your covenant and keep your promises of unfailing love to those who love You and obey Your commands. … ⁹But the Lord our God is merciful and forgiving, even though we have rebelled against Him.*

> **Appreciate:** One of the best ways to come near to the heart of God is to give Him thanks and recount how—consistent with His character—He has been good to you in the past.

4. *But we have sinned and done wrong. We have rebelled against You and scorned Your commands and regulations. We have refused to listen to Your servants the prophets, who spoke on Your authority to our kings and princes and ancestors and to all the people of the land. Lord, You are in the right; but as You see, our faces are covered with shame. This is true of all of us, including the people of Judah and Jerusalem and all Israel, scattered near and far, wherever You have driven us because of our disloyalty to You. O Lord,*

*we and our kings, princes, and ancestors are covered
with shame because we have sinned against You...
¹⁰ We have not obeyed the Lord our God, for we have
not followed the instructions He gave us through His
servants the prophets. All Israel has disobeyed Your
instruction and turned away, refusing to listen to Your
voice. So now the solemn curses and judgments written
in the Law of Moses, the servant of God, have been
poured down on us because of our sin. You have kept
Your word and done to us and our rulers exactly as
You warned. Never has there been such a disaster as
happened in Jerusalem. Every curse written against
us in the Law of Moses has come true. Yet we have
refused to seek mercy from the Lord our God by turning from our sins and recognizing His truth. Therefore, the Lord has brought upon us the disaster He
prepared. The Lord our God was right to do all of
these things, for we did not obey Him. O Lord our
God, You brought lasting honor to Your name by rescuing Your people from Egypt in a great display of
power. But we have sinned and are full of wickedness.*

> **Acknowledge:** As we can see, the bulk of Dan-
> iel's prayer is focused on confession. Here,
> Daniel not only confesses his sins but also the

sins of his kinsmen, the nation, and the leaders of the people. Daniel also acknowledges God's right to judge and how God has rightly followed through on His previous warnings.

5. *In view of all Your faithful mercies, Lord, please turn Your furious anger away from Your city Jerusalem, Your holy mountain. All the neighboring nations mock Jerusalem and Your people because of our sins and the sins of our ancestors. O our God, hear Your servant's prayer! Listen as I plead. For Your own sake, Lord, smile again on Your desolate sanctuary. O my God, lean down and listen to me. Open Your eyes and see our despair. See how Your city—the city that bears Your name—lies in ruins. We make this plea, not because we deserve help, but because of Your mercy. O Lord, hear. O Lord, forgive. O Lord, listen and act! For Your own sake, do not delay, O my God, for Your people and Your city bear Your name.*

> **Ask:** Even though the confessions in the Acknowledgement portion of Daniel's prayer are true, accurate, and deserved, here, Daniel is bold and specific in His ask of God. Daniel is also pointing out the reasons he believes

he can ask for these things: God's faithfulness (vs.16); God's mercy (vs. 16 and 18); God's love for Jerusalem, His holy mountain (vs. 16); and for the sake of God's reputation (vs. 17 and 19).

Notice how Daniel invited God to act!

From the subsequent passages, we know that Daniel followed through with his actions and commitment to be faithful. After he prayed, he acted.

NEHEMIAH'S PRAYER

Another example is the prayer of Nehemiah following the news that the holy city of Jerusalem had fallen into disrepair. He went to God and prayed the following prayer found in Nehemiah 1:5-11:

> [5] Then I said,

> "O LORD, God of heaven, the great and awesome God who keeps His covenant of unfailing love with those who love Him and obey His commands, [6] listen to my prayer! Look down and see me praying night and day for Your people Israel. I confess that we have sinned against You. Yes, even my own family and I have sinned! [7] We

have sinned terribly by not obeying the commands, decrees, and regulations that You gave us through Your servant Moses.

[8] "Please remember what You told Your servant Moses: 'If you are unfaithful to Me, I will scatter you among the nations. [9] But if you return to Me and obey My commands and live by them, then even if you are exiled to the ends of the earth, I will bring you back to the place I have chosen for My name to be honored.'

[10] "The people You rescued by Your great power and strong hand are Your servants. [11] O Lord, please hear my prayer! Listen to the prayers of those of us who delight in honoring You. Please grant me success today by making the king favorable to me. Put it into his heart to be kind to me."

In those days I was the king's cup-bearer.

Now, again, let's look at this prayer according to the six phases we've discussed.

1. *Lord,*

> **Align:** Not only is this a common and succinct salutation, using the word "Lord" is also

a statement of alignment. This word shows deference and a willingness to come under the authority—the lordship—of another, in this case, The LORD God.

2. *God of heaven, the great and awesome God who keeps His covenant of unfailing love with those who love Him and obey His commands,*

> **Adore:** After asserting His Lordship, it is only fitting that Nehemiah then praises God for who He is and what He has done.

3. *listen to my prayer! Look down and see me praying night and day for Your people Israel.*

> **Ask:** Such a simple and yet profound request: that the Lord God of Heaven would listen to and see Nehemiah. This is the first ask Nehemiah makes.

4. *I confess that we have sinned against You. Yes, even my own family and I have sinned! We have sinned terribly by not obeying the commands, decrees, and regulations that You gave us through Your servant Moses.*

> **Acknowledge:** Nehemiah does not hold back.

He readily acknowledges his sin and that of his
relatives. He also is clear that his sin is against
God. You can hear the grieving in his heart.

5. *Please remember what You told Your servant Moses:
'If you are unfaithful to Me, I will scatter you among
the nations. But if you return to Me and obey My
commands and live by them, then even if you are
exiled to the ends of the earth, I will bring you back
to the place I have chosen for My name to be honored.'*

*The people You rescued by Your great power and strong
hand are Your servants. O Lord, please hear my prayer!
Listen to the prayers of those of us who delight in honoring You. Please grant me success today by making
the king favorable to me. Put it into his heart to be
kind to me.*

Ask: Nehemiah makes his second request.
He also reminds God of His previous promises and His faithfulness in the past. And, in
the midst of his ask, he also inserts adoration
(that God is the One with great power and
a strong hand) and acknowledgement (that
He is the rescuer). In his final statements, he
also makes it clear that he plans to act and

asks God to give him favor and to affect the heart of king Artaxerxes.

6. *In those days I was the king's cup-bearer.*

> **Act:** The note left at the end of this prayer—that Nehemiah was cup-bearer to the king—is not just an ancillary factoid. It is a declaration that Nehemiah was prepared to use his position to act on what the Lord had laid on his heart. And he was trusting God to put it in the king's heart to be kind to him, as Nehemiah requested at the end of verse 10.

Nehemiah's prayer is a good reminder that while the order of the six phases laid out in this approach is a logical progression, your prayer life should not be prescriptive. Just like Nehemiah, you should pray as the Holy Spirit leads.

JESUS' GARDEN PRAYER

Finally, in the garden of Gethsemane, our precious Lord prayed to His Heavenly Father. We will examine the passage recorded in Mark 14:36.

> "Abba, Father," he cried out, "everything is possible for you. Please take this cup of suffering

away from me. Yet I want your will to be done, not mine."

The following table shows how the model is present even in this short prayer:

1. *Abba,*

> **Appreciate:** This is a term of love, appreciation, and endearment similar to the American English word, daddy.

2. *Father,*

> **Align:** Just as we discussed in The Lord's Prayer, this clause in the prayer is where He recognizes that God is His Father, representing an authority over Him. Jesus is intentionally aligning under the headship and authority of His Father.

3. *everything is possible for You.*

> **Adore:** Jesus is rightly attesting to Father God's rightful sovereignty, power, and ownership over all things, including Jesus' current and pending circumstances.

4. *Please take this cup of suffering away from me.*

> **Ask:** Jesus is making His request to Father
> God. Jesus knew why He came. Jesus knew
> His assignment, so He knew that He had to
> go through the suffering and death that was
> before Him. Yet, in His beautiful humanity,
> He asks His Father for what was surely not
> possible. There is no sin or shame in present-
> ing our requests to God if we humble our-
> selves under His authority and acknowledge
> that we ultimately want His will to prevail,
> which Jesus does next.

5. *Yet I want Your will to be done, not mine.*

> **Acknowledge:** It is this statement—His abso-
> lute resignation to the will of God—which
> made possible everything else that followed.
> Jesus agreed with God, laid down His natu-
> ral power to rescue Himself, and committed
> to the cross. (Praise be to Jesus!)

And we know Jesus followed up this prayer with action as
He went to the cross and rose again. He left this prayer encoun-
ter and immediately followed through on His next steps.

These are just four examples. Throughout the Bible there are many other examples of powerful prayers based on these six phases of genuine intimacy and connection with God.

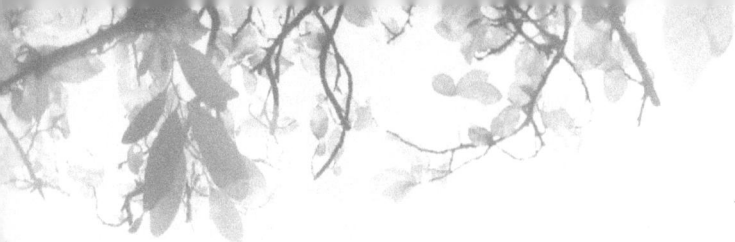

HOW TO USE THIS BOOK

My sons, do not neglect your duties any longer!
The Lord has chosen you to stand in His presence,
to minister to Him, and to lead the people
in worship and present offerings to Him.

2 CHRONICLES 29:11

This powerful prayer approach is not intended to be confining or prescriptive. It is intended to breathe fresh life into your time with God by illuminating elements of prayer which may be currently missing, ineffective, or stale.

It is best to use all six phases in succession. If you do, you will find that your prayer life—and your connection with the heart of God—will become richer, more satisfying, and more effective. Your prayer does not need to be long to be effective, and this approach may be done either in a brief time of prayer or during an extended time of communion with God.

An alternate way of using this book, especially when first starting, is to focus on incorporating or expanding one phase at a time. Below are just a few examples.

INTENTIONAL **ALIGNMENT**:

- Ask God to make your heart and mind genuinely in alignment with His. (Philippians 2:5)

- Look for ways throughout the day that you can re-align your heart with His. (1 Chronicles 16:11)

- Ask Him to show you where His heart is throughout the day—for people, for circumstances, and in your to-do list. (Proverbs 3:5-6)

ACCENTUATE **ADORATION**:

- You can never praise him too much. (Psalm 34:1-3; Psalm 103:1-4)

- The end of Ephesians 1:14 tells us that we were created, adopted, chosen, and redeemed so that we would praise and glorify Him!

Linger in **APPRECIATION**:

- Consider all He is and has done for you. (James 1:17)

- Expand upon what you have to be thankful for to include the people in your life, your job, your home, your neighborhood, your nation, the world, creation, etc. I guarantee that you cannot come to the end of things for which to thank Him. (1 Thessalonians 5:16-18)

Spend more time **ACKNOWLEDGING**:

- Your sins—spend extra time asking God to reveal any hidden sins. (Psalm 19:12-13; Psalm 139:23-24; 1 John 1:9; Romans 6:23)

- The sins of the nations. (Proverbs 14:34)

- The sins of humanity. (Romans 3:23; Isaiah 59:2; Romans 6:23)

- Genuine saving faith in Jesus is the only way to reconciliation with God. (Romans 10:9-10)

- His will is better than yours. (Luke 22:42)

EXPAND YOUR **ASK** PHASE
TO GO BEYOND YOURSELF AND
IMMEDIATE CIRCUMSTANCES, PRAY FOR:

- The nations—God's heart is that all people would come to know, love, and follow Jesus. (2 Peter 3:9)

- The peace of Jerusalem. (Psalm 122)

- The Jewish people to return to the Lord and accept Jesus as their long-awaited Messiah. (Micah 7:18-20)

- Believers who are being persecuted for their faith in Christ. (Hebrews 13:3; Matthew 5:10-12; Revelation 2:10)

- Peace between nations. (Matthew 5:9; Psalm 29:11)

- National, state, and local civic leaders. (Proverbs 11:14; 1 Timothy 2:1-2)

- Your church and pastors. (1 Thessalonians 5:12-13)

- Good stewardship of our natural resources. (Genesis 1:26-28)

- For animals to be treated properly. (Proverbs 12:10)

- The Bible's translation and transportation to reach all people hungry for the Word of God. (Matthew 28:18-20; Isaiah 52:7)

You can also look up scriptures that coincide with each of the phases. Read them during your prayer time and even pray the scriptures back to God. Scripture reading as part of daily time with God is also important for communion with God and spiritual growth. Remember that His word will not return to Him empty, but it will always accomplish His purposes (Isaiah 55:11).

The approach is very simple. Once you have become familiar with the phases and the approach, you can easily teach the approach in your Sunday School classes, create a song around it to help kids and youth (and adults) remember the phases and enrich their own prayer time.

Use the approach in corporate times of prayer at your church or in your small group.

Whatever you do, keep genuinely connecting with the heart of God!

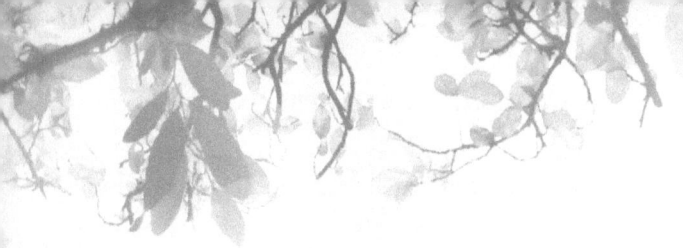

CHAPTER 10

A FINAL WORD

*Hear my prayer, O God; listen
to the words of my mouth.*

PSALM 54:2 NIV

I hope this little book has been helpful to you. I have been praying for you and asking God to transform your prayer life into a vibrant, fulfilling discourse of love. Prayer can be as natural and necessary as taking your next breath.

Prayer should not be a rote exercise but rather a personal, individual conversation in your own words. Therefore, I decided not to include full sample prayers because they would be prayers in my words not yours.

Please don't let this overwhelm you or feel daunting in any way, for that is a tactic of the enemy to cause you to not pray at all. Again, prayer is just a conversation between two persons who love each other. All you need is a heart long-ing to connect—no special words, fancy title, or elaborate attire needed.

I pray that talking with your loving, gracious, Heavenly Father would become one of your very favorite things to do.

...so as to walk in a manner worthy of the Lord, fully pleasing to Him: bearing fruit in every good work and increasing in the knowledge of God;

COLOSSIANS 1:10 ESV

NOTES

1. "Align." Merriam-Webster.com Dictionary, Merriam-Webster, https://www.merriam-webster.com/dictionary/align. Accessed 18 Jan. 2023.

2. Hatch, Tracy, *Finally Free — The Forgiveness Lifestyle Participant Workbook,* Metamorphoō Press, 2022, 2023.

3. "Adore." Merriam-Webster.com Dictionary, Merriam-Webster, https://www.merriam-webster.com/dictionary/adore. Accessed 18 Jan. 2023.

4. "Appreciate." Merriam-Webster.com Dictionary, Merriam-Webster, https://www.merriam-webster.com/dictionary/appreciate. Accessed 23 Apr. 2023.

5. "Acknowledge." Merriam-Webster.com Dictionary, Merriam-Webster, https://www.merriam-webster.com/dictionary/acknowledge. Accessed 23 Apr. 2023.

6. "Act." Merriam-Webster.com Dictionary, Merriam-Webster, https://www.merriam-webster.com/dictionary/act. Accessed 23 Apr. 2023.

ABOUT ONETEN MINISTRIES

OneTen Ministries, based on Colossians 1:10, is a 501(c)(3) not-for-profit ministry on a mission to equip and inspire Christians to know, love, and follow Jesus as both Savior and Lord.

We achieve this through the four components the Apostle Paul prayed about in Colossians 1:10, that we would:

- Walk in a manner worthy of the Lord,
- Please Him in all respects,
- Bear fruit in every good work, and
- Increase in the knowledge of God.

Among a variety of free resources, OneTen Ministries offers the **Finally Free** course. This is a powerful retreat-style experience focused on the freedom found by embracing a lifestyle of forgiveness. This teaching is truly life changing.

Learn more and join us on the journey at
OneTenMinistries.com

ABOUT ENOUGHLIFE.COM

*Are you tired of striving and straining to achieve
more or afford more but find little genuine
peace and satisfaction in the achievement?*

*Are you paying a high personal price to attain
or maintain the stereotypical dream?*

Are you plagued by regrets?

*Do you carry the weight of expectations,
both yours and the expectations of others?*

What if, rather than striving and straining you could find true, lasting satisfaction and peace? It is possible! It's not about settling for less. It's about finding the perfect, peaceful place of exactly enough of all you truly desire.

The EnoughLife.com community exists to help all people learn to trade regret and expectation for the perfectly abundant life they were meant to live. This site explores how living in the sweet spot of enough can truly add peace, joy, value, and satisfaction to life.

No expectations, no shame. Come as you are. You are safe here. You are welcome here. Here, *you* are **Enough**!

Visit **EnoughLife.com** to learn more.

LOOKING FOR A DYNAMIC SPEAKER
FOR YOUR NEXT EVENT?

Tracy Hatch is a dynamic and experienced speaker who effectively engages with audiences while delivering powerful messages. Tracy has a large selection of messages to choose from, or request a custom message based on your own topic. Existing topics include a variety of biblical messages and leadership topics.

Tracy is also an engaging trainer, specializing in the topic of freedom through forgiveness.

Visit **TracyHatch.com** to learn more or to connect with Tracy about speaking at your next event.